Original title:
Knurled Branches Over the Silver Loop

Author: Aron Pilviste
ISBN HARDBACK: 978-1-80559-083-5
ISBN PAPERBACK: 978-1-80559-582-3

Transcendent Forms Wrapped in Silver's Kiss

Beneath the moon's soft, glowing light,
Whispers of dreams take gentle flight.
Silver shadows dance and play,
Eclipsing night, birthing day.

In twilight's hush, the world stands still,
Wrapped in beauty, the heart can fill.
Forms of wonder twist and bend,
Time's own fabric begins to mend.

Celestial songs in the silent air,
Echoing love, tender and rare.
Every heartbeat, a cosmic thread,
Guiding the souls where they are led.

Glistening paths of stardust glow,
Mapping the journeys we do not know.
Transcendent visions, bold yet true,
Wrapped in silver, a timeless view.

Awake with dawn, the light will break,
Unraveling dreams with each heart's ache.
In every moment, a spark persists,
Silver's kiss in the morning mist.

Twisted Twilights Beneath the Glistening Arch

Twilight whispers with a gentle sigh,
Beneath the arch where shadows lie.
Colors blend, a painter's dream,
As stars emerge, a cosmic beam.

Leaves cascade in the cooling night,
Casting dreams in soft twilight.
Whirls of dusk in balmy air,
Embrace the glow, a moment rare.

Pastel hues of fading light,
Entwine with hope as day turns night.
A glistening arch, where dreams take flight,
In the embrace of coming night.

Voices murmur in gentle streams,
Past and present weave in dreams.
Twisted tales of days gone by,
Sing beneath the twilight sky.

Here our hearts can come alive,
Beneath the arch where wishes thrive.
In twisted twilights, we will dive,
To find the magic, to feel the drive.

Gnarled Limbs Against a Shimmering Sky

Gnarled limbs stretch toward the dusk,
Tracing tales in shadows husk.
Against the sky, a shimmering hue,
Whispers of old, of paths once true.

Branches twist like ancient thoughts,
In twilight's glow, the world is caught.
A shimmering dance of stars above,
Calls us back to dreams we love.

Silhouettes of life intertwine,
Against the sky, both dark and fine.
Echoes linger, hearts entwined,
Nature's secrets, gently mined.

The air is thick with whispered wishes,
Life unfolds in muted dishes.
Gnarled limbs against the twilight sky,
Speak of journeys gone awry.

In the shimmer of the fading light,
We see the shadows take their flight.
Gnarled limbs remind us to explore,
The beauty found in aged folklore.

Nature's Veins Woven in Moonlight

Moonlight spills on a silken stream,
Nature's veins pulse, alive with dream.
Woven paths of silver glow,
Lead us deeper into the flow.

We wander where the shadows play,
In moonlit dances, night turns day.
Veins of nature softly beat,
With mystic hymns beneath our feet.

Ghostly whispers through the trees,
Carried gently on the breeze.
Each rustle sings of ancient lore,
As leaves conspire to share more.

In this embrace of night's caress,
Nature's heart reveals its dress.
Woven tales of joy and strife,
Bathed in moonlight, alive with life.

Together we walk in whispered light,
Through nature's veins, pure and bright.
In moonlit realms, our spirits soar,
Woven in dreams forevermore.

The Dance of Shadows on Silver Streams

On silver streams, shadows prance,
Each ripple starts a fleeting dance.
Moonlit waters, a mirror's embrace,
Reflect the secrets of time and space.

Whispers float on gentle tides,
Where every shadow softly glides.
Underneath the starlit sky,
The world awakens, breathes a sigh.

Ebon wings brush the shimmering hue,
In this ballet where dreams come true.
The dance unveils the night's delight,
As shadows quiver, hearts take flight.

Silver streams are alive with sighs,
Beneath the watchful, twinkling eyes.
Nature's rhythm, a soothing balm,
In every shadow, peace and calm.

Join the dance, let spirits rise,
On silver streams, under twilight skies.
Hold the moment, let it gleam,
The dance of shadows, a waking dream.

Celestial Dreams Woven in Knotted Petals

In the garden where light bleeds,
Petals whisper secrets of the stars.
Moonlight dances on tender finds,
While shadows weave through fragrant boughs.

Glistening dew on silk-spun dreams,
Colors blend in a soft embrace.
Nature's heart pulses, gently sways,
Underneath the night's tranquil gaze.

Each bloom holds tales of distant lands,
In their folds, magic softly dwells.
Knotted paths lead on to wonder,
Where whispers linger, time compels.

As twilight drapes in velvet tone,
Dreams entwine like a silken thread.
The universe hums in harmony,
Filling hearts where silence led.

Amongst the blooms, a song emerges,
Echoing through the silent night.
Woven deep in knotted petals,
Celestial visions take their flight.

Silvery Luminance on Twisting Trails

On twisting paths where moonlight weaves,
Gentle whispers of the night arise.
Silvery beams dance on the leaves,
Beneath a blanket of starry skies.

The forest breathes a tranquil tune,
Each step taken, a secret shared.
Luminance glows, bright as the moon,
In shadows deep, the heart is bared.

Glimmers catch on hidden streams,
Reflecting tales of ages past.
Nature's canvas, painted dreams,
Each brushstroke an echo, unsurpassed.

Finding solace in simple sights,
The trails twist like a woven thread.
In the hush, the world ignites,
With silvery tales that gently spread.

Beneath the branches, shadows play,
Illuminated by the night's grace.
On twisting trails, we find our way,
Luminance brightens every space.

Shadows Played on Roughened Bark

In the wood, shadows stretch and sway,
Roughened bark holds the stories close.
Echoes of time in rugged play,
Nature whispers what matters most.

Each gnarled line tells of the years,
Seasons shift with each passing breeze.
Beneath the surface, life appears,
A dance of dreams in ancient trees.

Sunlight filters through the leaves,
Patterns flicker like a silent song.
In the stillness, every heart believes,
That shadows played where we belong.

Nature's canvas, rich and deep,
As sunlight bathes the forest floor.
In every shadow, secrets keep,
Roughened bark holds tales of lore.

With each step, the echoes grow,
The woods alive with memories stark.
In stillness, let your spirit flow,
Where shadows played on roughened bark.

Elongated Dreams Amongst Twisted Growth

In a garden of twisted vines,
Elongated dreams reach for the sun.
Nature's fingers, where hope aligns,
Whisper of journeys yet begun.

Each tendril bends with graceful ease,
Seeking out the light's warm embrace.
Amongst the growth, the heart finds peace,
In tangled paths, a hidden space.

Fluttering leaves tell stories old,
Of secret worlds beneath the sky.
Windswept tales, in colors bold,
Invite the spirit to soar high.

As the dusk wraps the earth in gold,
Elongated dreams stretch wide and free.
In every twist, a mystery told,
Amongst the growth, we find our plea.

With every breath, the night unfolds,
A symphony in muted tone.
In twisted paths, our fate beholds,
Elongated dreams we call our own.

The Lattice of Twilight and Branching Paths

In twilight's embrace, shadows grow tall,
A web of choices, where whispers call.
Each path diverges, yet none stand still,
The night unveils what hearts may instill.

Fingers of dusk weave tales so fine,
Beneath fading stars, our dreams entwine.
We wander on roads, both old and new,
The lattice of fate guides each view.

Moments cascade like leaves in the breeze,
Carried away with comforting ease.
Each step we take, a delicate dance,
In twilight's glow, we find our chance.

Fragments of Light Through Twisted Grains

In fields where shadows twist and twine,
Fragments of light in an endless line.
Golden hues dappling under the sun,
A mosaic of dreams where once there was none.

The grains whisper secrets, ancient and bold,
Stories of courage, legends retold.
A dance of the past, woven through time,
In each humble stalk, a rhythm, a rhyme.

With fingers caressing the sunlit strands,
We gather the echoes in fertile lands.
Each moment a heartbeat, each breath a song,
In the tapestry's weave, we all belong.

Secrets of the Winding Arbor

Beneath the boughs where silence is deep,
Secrets of nature, the whispers keep.
The winding arbor, a haven for thought,
Holds tales of the old that time forgot.

With every rustle, a story unfolds,
Of creatures and dreams, of the brave and the bold.
The roots intertwine like hearts in a tale,
Each twist and turn, a mystery frail.

In shadows cast by the dancing leaves,
The heart finds solace, the spirit believes.
Through the winding path, we lose and we find,
The secrets held close, forever entwined.

The Dance of Vine and Moonlit Flow

In gardens where vines reach for the sky,
The moonlight dances, a soft lullaby.
Petals embrace the cool evening air,
In the glow of the night, dreams linger there.

Twisting like laughter, the tendrils do sway,
Under the stars that light up the way.
A rhythm of night, a serenade sweet,
Nature's own music, a fragrant retreat.

With every heartbeat, the shadows align,
Embracing the space where the world feels divine.
The dance of the vine, a story in bloom,
In moonlit flow, all darkness finds room.

Reflections of Light in Woodland Veins

Sunlight dapples through the leaves,
Whispers of woods in gentle breeze.
Shadows dance on dew-kissed ground,
Nature's heartbeats all around.

Streams of gold on emerald blades,
Each moment fleeting, memory fades.
In the silence, stories rest,
Where the woodland's spirit is best.

Colors flicker in the shade,
Crafting shapes that never fade.
Time suspends, a dream-like flight,
Revealing secrets in pure light.

Footsteps soft on ancient bark,
Echoes of life, a hidden spark.
In this realm, the soul takes wing,
In tranquil whispers, we will sing.

Under the boughs, we find our place,
Within this magic, a warm embrace.
Together lost, we shall explore,
The reflections of light, forevermore.

The Glistening Burst of Nature's Kin

Morning breaks with gentle grace,
Nature's kin in every place.
Petals glisten, colors glow,
Life awakens, soft winds blow.

Butterflies flit from bloom to bloom,
In the air, sweet floral perfume.
Each heartbeat syncs with nature's song,
In this moment, we belong.

The forest floor, a quilt of green,
Every shadow, a world unseen.
Joy erupts like springtime rain,
In every drop, a sweet refrain.

In the glades, the sunlight streams,
Casting light upon our dreams.
We wander forth, hand in hand,
United here in nature's land.

Life's canvas, vibrant and grand,
Touching hearts with gentle hands.
In every breath, we find our kin,
In nature's burst, our souls begin.

Winding Roots in the Ethereal Night

Under stars that softly gleam,
Whispers echo like a dream.
Moonlight weaves through tangled vines,
In this dark, the mystery shines.

Winding roots in hidden paths,
Nature's art, a spell that lasts.
The night unfolds, a velvet sheet,
Where shadows fold and silence meets.

In the coolness, whispers stir,
Songs of crickets softly purr.
A gentle rustle, leaves unite,
In the symphony of night.

Through the woods, we take our flight,
Tracing contours in the night.
The moon above, a silver guide,
As through the trees, our dreams reside.

Each step taken, quiet grace,
In this ethereal, sacred space.
Roots entwined, we find our way,
In the night, together, we stay.

A Veil of Silver Over Ancient Arms

In the twilight's soft embrace,
Ancient trees, a timeless space.
A veil of silver drapes the land,
Whispers of stories, soft and grand.

Branches reach like open hands,
Guardians of forgotten lands.
Underneath, the secrets lie,
Calling forth the stars on high.

Moonbeams wrap the world in light,
Softly kissing the edge of night.
Amidst the shadows, life survives,
In ancient arms, the spirit thrives.

Echoes of those who came before,
In the silence, we explore.
Their voices linger in the air,
A sacred trust, a timeless care.

A tapestry of dreams so wide,
Beneath the boughs, we will abide.
With every breath, a union charms,
A veil of silver over ancient arms.

Kiss of Twilight on Branching Currents

The sun dips low, the sky ignites,
A gentle hush, soft-hearted nights.
Rippling waves embrace the shore,
Whispers linger, forevermore.

Branches sway in evening's grace,
Casting shadows, a warm embrace.
Underneath the twilight glow,
Secrets murmur, soft and slow.

Reflections dance on water's face,
Lost in time, a fleeting trace.
As dusk descends and stars align,
The world feels tender, pure, divine.

Echoes fade into the night,
Guided by the silver light.
Nature sings, a sweet refrain,
In twilight's arms, we find our gain.

Patterns Lost in the Wilderness

Branches intertwine and weave,
Nature hides, we dare believe.
Footsteps soft on mossy ground,
Whispers lost, yet sorrow's found.

Patterns carved by time's own hand,
Hidden truths in shifting sand.
Every leaf tells tales untold,
Zephyrs carry dreams of old.

A symphony of rustling trees,
Melodies ride the evening breeze.
In the wild, the soul finds flight,
Guided home by starlit night.

Memories fade like soft-edged mist,
All that remains is nature's kiss.
In the depths of green we roam,
Seeking solace, finding home.

Chasing Reflections in Gnarled Dreams

In the woods where shadows dwell,
Twisted paths weave magic's spell.
Whispers drift through ancient trees,
Carrying tales on the breeze.

Gnarled limbs reach for twilight's glow,
As moonlight paints the world below.
Reflections shimmer, soft and bright,
Echoing dreams in the still night.

Footprints lead to the unknown,
A quest for truths we've never shown.
Chasing visions, hearts aflame,
Finding solace in the game.

Moments caught like fireflies,
Fleeting, bright, beneath the skies.
In the dance of dreams we find,
A world reflecting our own mind.

Enchanted Boughs Beneath the Silver Dome

Beneath the stars, the whispers flow,
Enchanted boughs in moonlight glow.
Nature's arms embrace the night,
Weaving dreams in soft twilight.

Silver dome, a sheltering grace,
Starlit paths, a sacred space.
Where shadows blend with light so sweet,
And hearts awaken, skipping beat.

Through the leaves, the night winds sigh,
Echoes linger, a lover's cry.
In the silence, magic stirs,
In harmony, the universe purrs.

Each moment feels like timeless flight,
In the dark, everything feels right.
Enchanted dreams, they softly gleam,
Under the dome of silver beam.

Twinkling Memories Beneath Jagged Canopies

In the twilight's embrace, shadows play,
Whispers of laughter echo today.
Beneath the jagged, ancient trees,
Twinkling memories dance on the breeze.

Light spills through leaves in a gentle cascade,
Each flicker a story, together they wade.
The forest holds secrets, both old and true,
In the heart of the wild, I remember you.

Time slows in the hush of the emerald glade,
Every rustle of branches, a serenade.
Moments suspended in this sacred space,
Twinkling memories, time cannot erase.

A sigh of the world, a song softly sung,
The beauty of youth forever among.
In the depths of my heart, I carry the light,
Twinkling memories, my soul's delight.

Here, under canopies, we become one,
Two hearts intertwined, forever begun.
The night wraps us close in its silken thread,
Twinkling memories, in dreams they are fed.

The Weaving of Light Through Nature's Knuckles

In the dawn's tender glow, shadows unfurl,
Threads of gold weave through the world's swirl.
Nature's knuckles, rugged and wise,
Hold the whispers of life in disguise.

Rays filter gently through the tall pines,
Painting the earth with divine, silken lines.
A dance of the light, a flickering hope,
The weaving of magic, how trees learn to cope.

The sky blushes softly, a canvas anew,
While wildflowers nod, kissed by the dew.
Each petal a promise, each leaf a tale,
The weaving of light, a poignant trail.

Branches entwine as if held by fate,
Nature's embrace, both gentle and great.
In the stillness, a heartbeat resounds,
The weaving of light, where love abounds.

As dusk approaches, the colors entwine,
Silhouettes bloom in a crescent design.
The day gives its blessings, the night casts a spell,
The weaving of light, a story to tell.

Age-Worn Vines Beneath a Silvery Veil

In the quiet of dusk, where shadows lie,
Age-worn vines twist, as days pass by.
Beneath a silvery veil of soft mist,
Time weaves a story, too precious to miss.

Gentle whispers of leaves tell their tales,
Of seasons endured, of forgotten trails.
The embrace of the earth, a nurturing hand,
Age-worn vines thrive, eternally planned.

Each tendril a witness to life's flowing stream,
A tapestry woven, deep in a dream.
Beneath the soft glow of a moon's gentle light,
Age-worn vines shimmer, a beautiful sight.

Every twist and turn holds a memory's grace,
The lovers who danced in this sacred place.
They echo through time, both tender and bold,
Age-worn vines speak of stories untold.

In the night's tender arms, secrets they weave,
Under the stars, they sigh and believe.
Beneath a silvery veil, the magic is real,
Age-worn vines sing, their truths they reveal.

Eclipsed Echoes Beneath Nature's Frame

In twilight's embrace, an echo is cast,
Memories linger, both shadows and past.
Eclipsed by the trees, where silence remains,
Beneath nature's frame, a calmness sustains.

Whispers of time weave through the air,
Filling the silence, a gentle prayer.
Moonlight filters through branches above,
Eclipsed echoes murmur, a song of love.

The soft rustle of leaves stirs the night,
Carrying tales of forgotten light.
In the depths of the woods, dreams intertwine,
Eclipsed echoes tell of a life divine.

A symphony woven from dusk until dawn,
Nature's embrace, where all is reborn.
Melodies linger, throughout heart and soul,
Eclipsed echoes whisper, forever whole.

As stars gaze down with a wistful glance,
They join in the dance, the eternal romance.
Beneath nature's frame, every heartbeat aligns,
Eclipsed echoes carry through time's gentle shrines.

Silhouettes in Lunar Embrace

In shadows soft, we dance and sway,
The moonlight guides our secret play.
With whispers low, the night conceals,
Our silhouettes, as time reveals.

Beneath the stars, our bodies blend,
A cosmic touch, our spirits mend.
In every glance, the world must pause,
Embracing love, without a cause.

As silver beams on skin do trace,
We lose ourselves in vast embrace.
Connected souls in silent flight,
The night our canvas, pure delight.

The lunar glow, a gentle guide,
Through endless dreams, we drift and glide.
In moonlit realms, we find our home,
Forever wrapped in starlit foam.

A night of wonder, hearts entwined,
In every breath, our fate aligned.
In this embrace, we feel so free,
Silhouettes, just you and me.

Entangled Whispers Beneath a Glimmer

In twilight's hush, our voices stir,
Softly spoken, no need for blurr.
Amidst the glow, the secrets flow,
Entangled whispers, hearts aglow.

Beneath the stars, our dreams align,
Cascading tales, your hand in mine.
With every glance, the night draws near,
In glimmers small, love conquers fear.

The nightingale sings a haunting song,
Inviting us where we belong.
With gentle sighs, we fade as one,
In tangled rhythms, hearts have spun.

The silver sheen on leaves does cast,
Reflections of a love so vast.
With whispered thoughts that intertwine,
We dance as shadows, bright, divine.

Each tender touch, a spark ignites,
Illuminated by starry sights.
In every breath, we find our way,
Entangled whispers, night and day.

Serpentine Traces of Celestial Light

Through tangled paths where shadows creep,
We find the traces, secrets keep.
In swirling spirals, dreams take flight,
Serpentine dances in the night.

The stars align, a cosmic dance,
In every glance, the heart's expanse.
With every curve, we lose the fight,
To flow with love, a pure delight.

Each shimmering trail leads us close,
In whispered serenades, love flows.
Together bound in tender light,
Chasing echoes of the night.

The heavens paint our canvas wide,
As stardust wraps us, side by side.
In this embrace, we lose all fright,
Serpentine traces, shining bright.

With cosmic winds, we weave our fate,
In every pulse, we resonate.
In radiant paths, we step anew,
Chasing dreams, just me and you.

A Tangle of Dreams Under a Gleaming Crescent

Beneath the crescent, shadows play,
In tangled dreams, we drift away.
With every breath, the night descends,
A whispered tune that never ends.

In twilight's grace, our souls collide,
As visions blur, we will confide.
With moonlit beams that softly gleam,
We find ourselves inside a dream.

A world renewed by silver light,
Our spirits dance, embracing night.
In this embrace, our hearts align,
A tangle of dreams, so pure, divine.

The shadows stretch, their fingers grasp,
From reality, we gently clasp.
In twilight's fold, we cast away,
The doubts that linger, fade away.

Each secret shared beneath the glow,
With glimmers bright, our love will grow.
In crescent's arc, we find our way,
A tangle of dreams, come what may.

Tapestry of Night

In the hush of twilight skies,
Stars awaken, softly rise.
Veil of shadows, woven tight,
Crafts a tapestry of night.

Moonlight dances on the ground,
Whispers echo, all around.
Crickets sing a lullaby,
As the evening bids goodbye.

Gentle breezes kiss the trees,
Carrying secrets on the breeze.
Nature's heart begins to beat,
In the shadows, calm and sweet.

Dreams are painted, hues of blue,
In the night, a world anew.
Each bright star, a silent song,
Guides the weary soul along.

As the dawn begins to creep,
Nights we treasure, ours to keep.
In the light, the night will fade,
Yet in hearts, its magic stayed.

Whispered Leaves

In the forest, whispers flow,
Leaves converse, secrets they know.
Branches sway in soft embrace,
Nature's breath, a sacred space.

Underneath the canopy,
Lives a world, wild and free.
Every rustle, tales unfold,
Of ancient paths, both brave and bold.

Sunlight filters, gentle glow,
Casting shadows, long and low.
Roots entwined, stories share,
In their depths, a timeless care.

Through the seasons, truths remain,
Life's a cycle, joy and pain.
Whispered leaves, as they entwine,
Hold the whispers, yours and mine.

Though the world may shift and change,
Nature's heart, it won't estrange.
In the quiet, we can find,
Wisdom in the leaves, entwined.

Secrets Hanging from the Sky

Clouds drift softly, dreams above,
Carrying whispers of sweet love.
Secrets linger in the air,
Woven gently, everywhere.

Stars like lanterns, flicker bright,
Guide lost souls through endless night.
They speak softly, tales of old,
Of wishes made and hearts consoled.

Raindrops fall, a soothing sound,
In their cadence, peace is found.
Each drop carries, life anew,
A secret gift from skies so blue.

As the sun begins to rise,
Colors burst across the skies.
Secrets shining, day unfolds,
In the light, their truth beholds.

Look above and you will see,
Life's great tapestry, so free.
In each moment, take a sigh,
Find the secrets hanging nigh.

Currents of Time Beneath the Boughs

Underneath the ancient trees,
Time flows gently with the breeze.
Leaves tell stories, old and wise,
Secrets held where memory lies.

Roots entwined like whispered dreams,
Flowing softly, life redeems.
Around the trunk, the shadows play,
Marking moments, night and day.

Sunlight dances, flickers gold,
In its warmth, the tales unfold.
Beneath the boughs, time stands still,
Every heart knows nature's will.

Seasons shift like waves of tides,
In the stillness, peace resides.
Currents of time, both swift and slow,
Guide us where our spirits go.

So listen close, the world's refrain,
In the woods, joy lingers plain.
Life's a river, flowing free,
Currents of time, for you and me.

Flickers of Echoing Dreams

In the night, the stars will gleam,
Whispers wake, echoing dreams.
Thoughts like fireflies take their flight,
Dancing softly through the night.

Moments linger, fade away,
In their glow, shadows play.
Each dream flickers, soft and bright,
Painting canvas with the light.

From the depths of quiet hearts,
Voices rise, where hope imparts.
Echoes of what we hold dear,
Carrying warmth, feeling near.

In the silence, dreams are born,
Guiding lost souls, weary, worn.
Flickers of what we aspire,
Light the path to our desire.

As dawn breaks, the dreams retreat,
Yet in hearts, they hold their seat.
Flickers of love, forever streams,
Keep alive our echoing dreams.

Tapestry of Silver Interwoven with Tales

In quiet tones, the silver gleams,
Threads of fate weave subtle dreams.
Each glimmer holds a story true,
In whispers soft, the past breaks through.

A tapestry of night's embrace,
Woven tightly, every trace.
Time's gentle hand binds every strand,
Secrets held in fibers grand.

Beneath the shimmer, shadows play,
Lost in moments, fade away.
Every knot, a lesson learned,
Every turn, a passion burned.

A dance of light upon the dark,
Each flicker holds a quiet spark.
The tales it tells, forever vast,
A journey formed from future, past.

In silver threads, our fates entwine,
In every stitch, a life defined.
The tapestry, a living art,
Each woven tale, a beating heart.

The Space Between in Twisted Form

In shadows deep, a silence grows,
The space between, where longing flows.
Words unspoken, drift like dreams,
Caught in webs of fragile seams.

A twist of fate, a turn unplanned,
In fleeting time, we stretch our hands.
The distance felt, though close we stand,
A mystery we can't command.

Moments linger, heavy like clouds,
In the hush, our truth enshrouds.
Sparks ignited in quiet stares,
The weight of what's unsaid ensnares.

In the quiet, hearts collide,
In breaths held tight, the worlds divide.
Yearning held in gazes deep,
In this space, the secrets seep.

Twisted paths that fate designs,
In the space, our essence shines.
Bound by threads both frayed and worn,
In twisted form, new dreams are born.

Boughs of Silver Stretching to Eternity

Boughs of silver reach up high,
Kissed by stars that grace the sky.
In every leaf, a wish takes flight,
Soaring high into the night.

Branches bend, yet never break,
In their strength, the cosmos wakes.
Roots entwined in earth so deep,
Guarding secrets they will keep.

The gentle sway of whispered breeze,
Carries tales from ancient trees.
Time stands still; the moments blend,
In silver light, we find our end.

Echoes dance in moonlit glow,
Among the boughs, our spirits flow.
Each silver arc a path we tread,
With endless dreams that lie ahead.

To eternity, our hearts will climb,
Through branches woven, out of time.
In their embrace, we find our grace,
In silver boughs, a sacred space.

The Simmering Pulse Beneath Ancient Knots

Beneath the bark, a pulse does hum,
An ancient heart, where secrets churn.
Knots entwined in whispered lore,
A history held in roots galore.

The simmering pulse of life unfolds,
In every ring, a story holds.
Through seasons worn and tempests strong,
In every twist, the echoes throng.

In shadows cast by sunlight's grace,
The dance of time leaves its trace.
Twisted forms speak of the years,
Through laughter, loss, and silent tears.

The ancient knots hold tight their tales,
Of courage found in fierce gales.
Each layer tells of battles fought,
In the heart, the lessons taught.

Beneath the surface, rhythms flow,
A legacy of life we know.
In every pulse, the past lives on,
In ancient knots, our spirits drawn.

Glistening Threads of Thought in Nature's Embrace

In the morning dew, secrets unfold,
Whispers of dreams, soft and bold.
Leaves dance gently, caught in a breeze,
Nature's embrace puts my mind at ease.

Colors entwine, a vibrant weave,
Each petal and stem, a story to perceive.
Sunlight glimmers on the forest floor,
Threads of thought, forever explore.

Streams babble softly, carrying sighs,
Reflecting the heart where true beauty lies.
With every rustle, a tale is told,
In nature's arms, life's wonders unfold.

Mountains loom high, ancient and wise,
Guardians of time that never disguise.
In their shadows, I find my place,
Glistening threads in the quiet space.

The world spins around, yet still I stand,
With nature as guide, I lend her my hand.
Boundless and free, together we grow,
In glistening threads, my thoughts overflow.

Light Shattering Through Tattered Growth

Sunlight fractures through the tangled leaves,
Piercing the shadows where silence weaves.
Each ray a promise, reaching out wide,
Finding the beauty where there once was pride.

Old branches bend with tales to share,
Weaving their wisdom in the open air.
Light shimmers softly on forgotten stones,
Awakening whispers in muted tones.

Moss carpets the ground like emerald dreams,
Absorbing the light that brightly gleams.
And in the cracks, life finds its way,
Tattered and torn, yet here it will stay.

With every beam, a story takes flight,
Illuminating darkness, igniting the night.
Through tattered growth, hope starts to rise,
A dance with shadows beneath the skies.

In the gentle glow, I feel it ignite,
The spirit of life, joyous and bright.
Light shattering forth, breaking the mold,
With every heartbeat, new tales are told.

The Silhouette of Time in Twisted Souls

In the silence of dusk, shadows extend,
A silhouette of time, twisting around the bend.
Whispers of moments, both fragile and vast,
Echoing softly of a turbulent past.

Each heartbeat lingers, a dance of the soul,
Amidst the darkness, we strive for control.
Twisted through fate, our paths intertwine,
In the depths of the night, the stars brightly shine.

Beneath the moon's gaze, secrets collide,
The essence of time, in shadows, we hide.
With every tick, memories unfold,
In twisted silhouettes, the tale is told.

Lives interwoven, a tapestry spun,
As we chase the dawn, still fearing the run.
In the textured hues of the night's cool breath,
The silhouettes beckon, a dance with death.

Yet through the dark, hope's echoes remain,
For love's gentle light can soften the pain.
In the silhouette of time, we find our way,
Twisted souls guiding us, come what may.

A Quantum Spin on Tangled Roots

Beneath the surface, roots intertwine,
In quantum dances, they gracefully align.
Life's energy spins in each hidden vein,
Tangled and twisted, yet never in vain.

Through the soil rich, their whispers flow,
Stories of struggle and strength they bestow.
Branches reach high, aspiring to thrive,
In this quantum realm, we're truly alive.

Each leaf unfurling, a note in the song,
In the symphony of life, where we all belong.
Time bends and swirls, a cosmic embrace,
In tangled roots, we find our place.

The universe pulses, a rhythm, a beat,
With every connection, the journey's complete.
In the dance of the atoms, our fates intertwine,
A quantum spin, our souls brightly shine.

And while storms may rage and shadows may call,
Strength lies in the roots, steadfast through all.
A quantum spin in this wondrous play,
Tangled and free, we shall find our way.

Whispers of Twisted Twigs

In the forest deep and wide,
Twisted twigs in shadows hide.
Whispers echo through the night,
Nature's secrets take to flight.

Beneath the moon's soft, pale glow,
Ancient stories come and go.
Branches sway, a gentle song,
In their dance, where souls belong.

Crickets chirp, their voices rise,
As stars twinkle in the skies.
The woods breathe with timeless grace,
In this sacred, hidden space.

Each rustling leaf, a sighing breath,
A reminder of life and death.
From the depths of earth to air,
Twisted twigs weave tales of care.

Winds carry forth the murmurs low,
In every nook, the stories flow.
Embrace the night, let spirits roam,
In the whispers, you've found a home.

Moonlit Trails of Woven Shadows

Underneath a sky of blue,
Moonlit paths will guide you through.
Woven shadows dance and play,
Leading hearts that lose their way.

A silver touch upon the ground,
Magic whispers all around.
Footsteps soft on grassy trails,
Love persists, and hope prevails.

Trees entwined in lunar light,
Secrets shared in quiet night.
Crickets sing their lullabies,
As butterflies drift through the skies.

Every twist and curve we take,
In this night, our hearts awake.
Drawn by shadows, we align,
Bound by whispers, yours and mine.

Together in this soft embrace,
We lose ourselves in timeless space.
With moonlit trails beneath our feet,
Our woven shadows will repeat.

Quirks of Gnarled Wood

In the heart of twisted trees,
Gnarled wood sways with gentle ease.
Each curve a tale, a memory,
Of seasons past and what will be.

Knots and bends, a work of art,
Nature's canvas, life's own heart.
Whispers carried on the breeze,
Speak of wisdom found in these.

Bark so rough yet warm to touch,
Holds the scars of life as such.
From roots that reach both wide and deep,
To branches high where dreamers leap.

Sunlight dapples through the leaves,
As time unfolds, my spirit weaves.
In the quirks of gnarled wood,
I find solace, understood.

With every gate, I wander near,
To stories told year after year.
Nature's beauty, vast and proud,
In gnarled wood, I feel the crowd.

Spirals in the Silver Gleam

In the night, the spirals rise,
Reflecting in the starry skies.
Silver gleams on waters calm,
Whispers dance like soothing balm.

Every wave, a gentle swirl,
Nature's heartbeat starts to twirl.
Silken threads of midnight blue,
Entwine the dreams that we pursue.

With each pulse, the world awakes,
As moonlit pathways softly shakes.
Winding paths that twist and bend,
Reveal the secrets held within.

In this spiral dance of fate,
We find the hands of time elate.
Guided by the silver sheen,
We dare to chase what could have been.

Together through this night we roam,
In spirals, we create our home.
Beneath the stars, forever dream,
In life's embrace, we gleam and beam.

The Dreaming Canopy Under Silver-Gilded Skies

Underneath the endless arcs,
Where shadows dance and whisper low,
The trees extend their leafy arms,
Embracing dreams as soft winds blow.

Stars above in twinkling grace,
Gilded silver, shimmering bright,
They weave a tapestry of night,
And cradle secrets held in space.

Soft murmurs reach the ear with ease,
Of rustling leaves and nightingale,
In this realm of gentle peace,
Where worries fade and hearts grow pale.

Each branch a tale of time unlaced,
Of love that's lost and found again,
In twilight's hold, the dreams embraced,
Within the canopy's domain.

So let us roam beneath this sky,
Where silver gilds the solemn trees,
In nature's arms, our spirits fly,
The dreaming canopy sets us free.

Moonlit Trails Winding Through Nature's Arms

Moonlit paths that softly gleam,
Guide us through the evening's lore,
With every step, a whispered dream,
In nature's arms, we long for more.

The trees stand tall, their shadows cast,
An echo of the silent night,
Each rustle speaks of journeys past,
Where every turn reveals delight.

Crickets sing a tune so sweet,
While fireflies dance like scattered stars,
With every breath, our hearts shall meet,
As magic lingers just for ours.

A winding trail through emerald friend,
Where paths entwine beneath the sky,
Each curve and bend, a brand new blend,
In moonlit glades, our spirits fly.

So let us stroll this endless way,
With twilight's glow as our embrace,
Through nature's arms, we find our play,
A dance with time, a sacred space.

Whispers of Old Wounds in Gleaming Light

In shadows deep, old wounds reside,
Whispers echo, tales of pain,
Yet gleaming light, a gentle guide,
Offers solace where hope regains.

Each scar a story, etched in time,
A testament of battles fought,
Yet through the cracks, the light will climb,
Transforming scars into what's sought.

The heart remembers, yet it heals,
Each whispered truth, a tender balm,
For in the light, the spirit feels,
A current of transcendent calm.

As dawn arrives with pastel hues,
The past dissolves in morning's glow,
These whispers fade, replaced by views,
Of brighter days and love to grow.

So let the healing touch our core,
With every breath, we rise anew,
In gleaming light, we shall restore,
The hope within, forever true.

Luminescent Patterns Among Twisted Forms

In twilight's grasp, the shadows twist,
Creating art in silent night,
Luminescent patterns dance and twist,
As forms emerge in fleeting light.

Winding branches, shapes that sway,
With glimmers bright, a haunting grace,
Illusions play in night's ballet,
Through tangled worlds, we seek a trace.

Each movement speaks a language soft,
Of beauty found in every flaw,
In crooked lines that lift us off,
To realms untouched by nature's law.

The moonlight paints a canvas rare,
With strokes of silver, bold yet free,
In twisted forms, we find a prayer,
A dance of wonder, endlessly.

So let us lose ourselves tonight,
In luminescence, dreams unfold,
Amongst the patterns, pure delight,
In nature's grace, our hearts are told.

Twilight's Embrace on Woodland Twists

In twilight's glow, the shadows dance,
Colors weave in a soft romance.
Whispers of leaves, a gentle sigh,
As day bids farewell to the sky.

Branches twist like timeless lore,
In the hush, a spirit soars.
Beneath the veil, secrets reside,
Where day and night gently collide.

Softly the stars begin to bloom,
Filling the woods with silvery gloom.
Each path leads to a hidden dream,
Where echoes of dusk softly gleam.

The air kissed by a fragrant breeze,
Carrying tales through ancient trees.
Night cradles the woodland tight,
In the arms of deepening night.

With every step, the heartbeats blend,
In twilight's arms, we gently mend.
Nature whispers its sweet refrain,
In twilight's embrace, we remain.

The Embrace of Time in Spiraled Form

Time entwined in spiraled grace,
A gentle touch, a soft embrace.
Moments held like precious dew,
Each glance reveal the old and new.

In winding paths, the ages flow,
Memories bloom like petals slow.
Circles drawn in the sands of years,
Through laughter bright and hidden tears.

The seasons change, yet shadows blend,
In this dance, we find no end.
Ticking clocks and whispered dreams,
Life unfolds in golden beams.

Every heartbeat tells a tale,
In this spiral, we prevail.
Threads of time both thin and wide,
In the embrace where spirits glide.

So let us cherish every turn,
In time's embrace, we softly yearn.
Each moment cherished, held so dear,
As we spiral through the years.

Shadows Curling Like Silver Threads

In twilight's reach, shadows weave,
Curling softly, we dare believe.
Silver threads in the fading light,
Whispers echoing deep in night.

They linger soft on the forest floor,
Like secrets hidden, forevermore.
Drawing close in the moon's gentle grace,
We find ourselves in this sacred space.

Each twist and turn tells a story bold,
Of lives entwined and journeys told.
These shadows dance with a silent song,
In their embrace, we all belong.

What mysteries hide in the winding dark?
Amidst the shadows, we find our spark.
Glistening threads bridge hearts and minds,
In the night's embrace, a truth unwinds.

So let us tread where shadows play,
In their curls, we lose our way.
Silver threads guide us near,
In twilight's arms, we have no fear.

Radiance Nestled in Gnarled Embrace

Amidst the gnarled trees that stand,
Radiance glows, an unseen hand.
Cradling light in a rustic nest,
Where nature's heart finds quiet rest.

Twisted branches cradle the sun,
Holding warmth before day is done.
Leaves shimmer like a painted dream,
In shadows deep, the softest gleam.

This dance of light, a fleeting kiss,
In tangled roots, we find our bliss.
Each moment's glow, a fleeting dance,
Inviting all to take a chance.

The forest whispers ancient names,
In their embrace, our spirit flames.
With every breath, the colors swirl,
In radiant tales, our hearts unfurl.

So let us linger where shadows meet,
In gnarled embrace, our souls complete.
Each glimmer holds a world anew,
In nature's arms, we find our hue.

Curved Paths of Radiance and Grit

In the valley where shadows meet,
The sun spills gold on the weary feet.
Each step forward, a promise to chase,
Carving new paths in a world of grace.

With dusk approaching the hills stand tall,
Whispers of courage in twilight's call.
Softly, the stars begin to ignite,
Guiding the hearts that seek the light.

Battles fought in the silence of night,
Resilience blooms, a fervent sight.
Through the thorns, the flowers emerge,
In every struggle, a hopeful surge.

The river flows with stories untold,
Of dreams once lost and now brave and bold.
Embracing the curves, we dance with fate,
United in purpose, we rise, we create.

In this journey, the echoes remain,
Of laughter, of joy, of shadowed pain.
The path of grit, with radiance bright,
Illuminates all in the soft moonlight.

Echoes of Twilight Amongst Twisted Wood

In the depths where the shadows blend,
The twilight whispers, a delicate friend.
Branches entwined like fate's gentle hand,
Echoes of secrets lost in the land.

Every rustle sings tales of the past,
Moments captured, memories cast.
Soft murmurs roam through the twilight air,
Weaving together the stories we share.

Beneath the canopy, stillness resides,
Where nature's beauty endlessly hides.
Through tangled paths, heartbeats entwine,
In the laughter of leaves, emotions align.

Violet hues brush the earth with grace,
As time dances gently, leaving no trace.
Among twisted roots, we find our way,
In harmony, fading night meets the day.

With each step forward, we honor the night,
Finding solace in shadows, a curious sight.
In the murmurs of twilight, we belong,
Threads of our dreams, woven in song.

Silver Threads of Time in Nature's Grasp

In the morning mist, time softly glows,
Silver threads shimmer where the wildflower grows.
Nature's embrace, a timeless caress,
Guiding our hearts towards sweet tenderness.

Every leaf tells a story of years,
Whispers of laughter, echoes of tears.
Seasons unfold in a vibrant dance,
Inviting our souls to take a chance.

Beneath the canopy, shadows may play,
But sunlight breaks through to show us the way.
Time weaves connections, both strong and frail,
In nature's tapestry, we shall not fail.

From roots that burrow to the skies above,
The dance of life sings of hope and love.
Silver threads spark in the morning light,
Framing our journey as day turns to night.

In every heartbeat, in every sigh,
Time flows like rivers, never asking why.
Within nature's grasp, we learn to trust,
Guided by starlight, in dreams we adjust.

Branches That Reach for Stardust

Underneath the vast celestial dome,
Branches reach out, yearning to roam.
With open arms they beckon the night,
Catching the dreams that shimmer with light.

In the stillness, whispers raise the sky,
Rustling leaves echo a gentle sigh.
Every star above, a wish unconfined,
Calling the hearts that dare to find.

Through gentle breezes, secrets are shared,
In the dance of the night, we are bared.
Each branch a story, a life intertwined,
Fingers of nature, seeking what's kind.

The moonlight settles like soft silver lace,
Kissing the branches in a loving embrace.
In the quiet expanse, we learn to trust,
Reaching for stardust, ourselves should we gust.

With every heartbeat, the forest stands tall,
Reaching for dreams that we hold through it all.
Bound by the magic of the night's soft glow,
We walk hand in hand, where wild wonders flow.

The Silken Orbit of Old Growth

In whispered woods where silence reigns,
Ancient trees sway with soft refrain.
Roots entwined in earthen lace,
Holding secrets time can't erase.

A canopy high where sunlight weaves,
Golden threads among the leaves.
Branches stretch in graceful arcs,
Guardians of long-forgotten marks.

Ferns flutter like whispers of dreams,
Nestled low where the daylight gleams.
Mossy carpets cradle each foot,
Softening steps where life takes root.

A dance of shadows, a tender sigh,
Time drifts slowly, as moments fly.
In this embrace of nature's birth,
The heart finds solace in the earth.

Endless stories in each ring told,
Of seasons' change and memories old.
The silken orbit of the past,
In the old growth, we find peace at last.

Serene Shadows Surrounding the Luminous Bend

In twilight's hush, the river flows,
Beneath the sky where soft light glows.
Serene shadows stretch and blend,
Whispers float, and moments suspend.

The water dances, gleams like glass,
Reflecting skies where echoes pass.
Gentle breezes swirl and twirl,
Caressing leaves, each strand unfurls.

Moonlight spills on the quiet bank,
Illuminated paths, a shimmering prank.
Stars peek down through branches wide,
A celestial guide by the riverside.

In this embrace, the world feels right,
Luminous bends in the velvet night.
Memories linger like soft caress,
In serene shadows, we find our rest.

Nature's hymn in the stillness sings,
Of tranquil hearts and gentle things.
Each ripple carries a timeless tune,
Under the watchful gaze of the moon.

Chronicles of Boughs and Celestial Circles

Among the boughs where stories breathe,
Chronicles written, weaves and sheathes.
Whispers linger from branch to sky,
Tales of the old that never die.

A twist of light through emerald leaves,
Holds shadows deep where time weaves.
Celestial circles overhead gleam,
As if nature herself wrote a dream.

Boughs arching high with wisdom old,
Each knot and split a memory told.
Stars alight like diamonds frail,
Guiding wanderers with their trail.

In this sanctuary, thoughts take flight,
Chasing echoes in the soft twilight.
Nature's narrative, a sacred scroll,
Crafted with whispers, heart, and soul.

Among these branches, we quietly stand,
Bound to the tales of this ancient land.
Chronicles of life through nature's art,
Written forever in the heart.

Murmurs of the Night Through Twisted Twigs

Beneath the cloak of an inky sky,
Murmurs rise where shadows lie.
Through twisted twigs, the night unfolds,
Carrying secrets that nature holds.

Each rustle speaks of things unseen,
Of quiet wonders that might have been.
Crickets serenade the moonlit air,
As starlit dreams twinkle with care.

A forest breathes, a living sigh,
Echoes linger where soft winds fly.
Branches speak in a silent loop,
To the nocturnal song of the hoop.

In this hushed realm where shadows play,
Life's mysteries dance, then drift away.
Whispers of magic and gentle things,
Fill the air as the nightbird sings.

Under the gaze of celestial light,
Murmurs weave through the velvet night.
Through twisted twigs, stories emerge,
In the stillness, our souls converge.

A Symphony of Light on Worn Limbs

In twilight's embrace, shadows dance slow,
Whispers of dreams in the evening glow.
Fingers trace paths of forgotten grace,
Worn limbs remember, in time, their place.

Under stars that flicker in the night,
Hope intertwines with each spark of light.
Carved by the years, each line tells a tale,
A symphony echoes, as spirits set sail.

Time's Embers Amongst Curved Edges

Time's gentle hand shapes curves divine,
Where edges soften like vintage wine.
Embers of moments in memories bright,
Drawing the past from the depths of night.

In every bend, a story concealed,
In whispered glances, our fates are revealed.
Time flows like water, reshaping the shore,
Amongst these edges, we seek evermore.

The Spell of Shimmering Twists and Turns

A winding path where secrets lie,
Shimmering twists beneath open sky.
Each footstep dances, a tale to unfold,
In the spell of the moment, our hearts turn to gold.

Like ribbons of light in a soft summer breeze,
we chase fleeting shadows, finding our ease.
The world spins gently, a delicate twirl,
In every circle, a new dream unfurl.

Fragile Silvers Beneath Mighty Arms

Fragile silvers, a breath of the past,
Beneath mighty arms, memories cast.
Holding the weight of what once was near,
Each glint a reminder of love and of fear.

In strength we find solace, tender yet bright,
Melding the shadows with shards of pure light.
Together we stand, come storms or calm days,
Navigating life in its intricate maze.

The Serpent's Path Through Whispering Woods

In shadows deep, the serpent slithers,
Through tangled roots where silence shivers.
Leaves rustle soft, a gentle sigh,
The woods awake, beneath the sky.

A winding trail, where secrets dwell,
Each curve and turn, a tale to tell.
Moonlight spills on the forest floor,
As whispers weave forevermore.

Echoes of night, the stars are near,
In every breath, the truth we hear.
The path unfolds with every step,
A dance of hope, where dreams are kept.

Through thickets dense, a light will break,
A guiding hand, for wanderers' sake.
The serpent leads, in twilight's breath,
Along the edge of life and death.

In nature's heart, where shadows part,
The journey blooms, a work of art.
Whispered winds in the trees will sigh,
The serpent's path beneath the sky.

Threads of Light in Tangled Silence

In muted hues, the dawn does creep,
Through tangled branches, dreams do leap.
A golden thread, like whispers spun,
Awakens life, invites the sun.

Beneath the hush of morning's grace,
We weave our thoughts in open space.
Reflections dance upon the streams,
Entwined with hope and fragile dreams.

Each glimpse of light, a story told,
In silent woods, where hearts unfold.
The gentle tug of nature's song,
Calls out to us, where we belong.

In shadows cast by ancient trees,
The threads of light sway with the breeze.
They speak in colors soft and bright,
Creating paths of pure delight.

Among the roots, where silence reigns,
The beauty lives, amidst the strains.
In tangled fibers, life takes flight,
Threads of light in the quiet night.

Murmurs of the Earthbound Sky

Beneath the arch of twilight's dome,
The earthbound sky calls us back home.
In whispers soft, the shadows play,
As night unfurls its dark bouquet.

A symphony of silent dreams,
In every twist, the starlight beams.
We listen close, to tales of old,
With every sigh, a truth unfolds.

From mountains high to valleys low,
The murmurs rise, in ebb and flow.
A dance of dust, a breath of air,
In every note, we find despair.

As echoes linger, stories fade,
The earthbound sky, in twilight laid.
We wander forth on softened ground,
In every heart, the whispers found.

The canvas dark, with stars that gleam,
Invites us deeper into dream.
In every murmur, we will fly,
To meet the light, the earthbound sky.

Entwined in Nature's Song

In forest depths, where shadows blend,
The songs of nature never end.
Each note a leaf, each breeze a rhyme,
In timeless dance, through space and time.

The chorus swells with every morn,
As dew drops glisten, fresh and worn.
The world resounds with vibrant tones,
In harmony, we call it home.

With whispers sweet, the flowers sway,
Their colors bright, they find their way.
In symphony, the wild takes flight,
Entwined in love, a pure delight.

The rustling grass, a soft refrain,
In every pulse, the earth's own pain.
Yet in the pain, a beauty grows,
In nature's song, the love still flows.

We close our eyes and breathe it in,
The joyful notes where hope begins.
Entwined in beauty, lost in throng,
Together we sing, we belong.

Whirling Illusions in the Woodland's Glow

In shadows deep where whispers play,
The leaves they dance, a soft ballet.
Moonlit trails on forest ground,
With every turn, new dreams are found.

Flickering lights like stars descend,
Nature's secrets in silence blend.
A symphony of rustling leaves,
Where magic lingers, heart believes.

The branches weave a tale anew,
Of creatures lost and those who flew.
Through tangled roots, the stories flow,
In woodland's heart, the mysteries grow.

Whispers echo through the night,
Guiding souls with pure delight.
A dance of shadows, deep and wide,
Where dreams and fears a dance abide.

As dawn approaches, colors blend,
The woodland's glow begins to end.
Yet in our hearts, the memories stay,
Of whirling visions, bright as day.

Nature's Lattice at Dusk's Decay

As twilight falls, the colors swirl,
A tapestry begins to unfurl.
The golden rays, like threads of gold,
In nature's loom, their stories told.

Crickets chirp a low refrain,
While shadows twist, as if in pain.
The sky, a canvas, brushes deep,
Where secrets of the night do creep.

Vines entwine like lovers lost,
In hushed embrace, they count the cost.
The iron scents of earth arise,
As dusk adorns the evening skies.

Beneath the trees, the tales are spun,
Of ancient deeds and battles won.
Nature's weave, so rich and vast,
Reminds us of our shadows cast.

In veins of twilight, echoes hum,
The night is here, the day is done.
Each moment trapped in threads of time,
A lattice formed, a silent rhyme.

Breathing Life into the Twisted Sky

A canvas stretched, so wild and free,
With hues of dusk, reality.
Clouds like whispers, drift and sway,
In dreams where wishes dare to play.

As stars awaken, stories rise,
From depths hidden in countless skies.
A symphony of light unfolds,
A dance of wishes, hopes retold.

In the quiet, a heartbeat hums,
As cosmic winds and laughter come.
Shadows wrap 'round fading light,
While mysteries bloom in velvet night.

Branches stretch like fingers wide,
Grasping at the stars with pride.
In nature's breath, the heavens sigh,
Awakening dreams that dance on high.

Life ignites the twisted shapes,
As night unveils its secret drapes.
Each glow a story, bold and bright,
Breathing life into the night.

Reflections on Flowing Shadows

A river winds, a mirror bright,
Reflecting dreams in dusky light.
As shadows dance upon the tide,
In every ripple, secrets hide.

The past unfolds in colors gray,
Where moments drift and fade away.
Echoes linger, soft and low,
In flowing whispers, time will show.

Leaves cascade like memories,
Carried forth on gentle breeze.
Their stories written on the stream,
Dissolving slowly, like a dream.

In twilight's grip, a hush descends,
As nature breathes, the river bends.
Each shadow shapes a tale anew,
Of everything we thought we knew.

Reflections fade as night arrives,
With quiet grace, the moment thrives.
In flowing shadows, life will seek,
The whispers of the nights we keep.

Spirals of Light and Twisted History

In the dusk where echoes swirl,
A tale unfolds, a silver pearl.
Whispers dance in the fading glow,
Twisted roots where secrets flow.

Ancient trees with gnarled limbs,
Cradle time in their quiet hymns.
Branches twist in a cosmic play,
Guiding dreams through night and day.

Stars flicker like distant minds,
Memories lost, yet love still binds.
In spirals bright, the past ignites,
Tracing paths of cosmic flights.

The heartbeats resonate with grace,
In every shadowed, sacred space.
Illuminated by the soul's desire,
Twisted tales that never tire.

A journey woven, your hand in mine,
Through spirals bright, where fates align.
Together we'll find what was concealed,
In the light, our truths revealed.

Night's Embrace over Time-Worn Branches

The moon casts silver on the leaves,
As night unveils what day believes.
Time-worn branches stretch and sigh,
In whispers soft beneath the sky.

Embracing shadows, dreams take flight,
Wrapped in the cloak of tender night.
Stars are the eyes that watch and wait,
For secrets held by twisted fate.

Each droplet of dew, a story spun,
Of battles lost and victories won.
Nature's breath, a gentle hymn,
Where night unfolds, and hopes begin.

The world slows down as senses heighten,
In dark corners where words are brightened.
Boughs arch low in a sacred dance,
Inviting souls to take a chance.

We wander through the quiet shade,
In the night's embrace, our fears allayed.
Time-worn tales of love and light,
Guide us home through the endless night.

Glimmers of Tomorrow on Wreathed Boughs

Glimmers twinkle where shadows play,
On boughs wreathed in the hues of gray.
Promises whisper in the breeze,
In every rustle, a dream to seize.

Morning breaks with colors bold,
Stories of hope waiting to unfold.
Each branch harbors a secret wish,
In nature's cradle, pure and swish.

The heart beats loud against the wood,
In quiet moments, a love that stood.
Swaying gently in rhythm's tune,
With glimmers of future, bright as noon.

A tapestry spun from light and form,
Crafting beauty amidst the storm.
On wreathed boughs, our dreams collide,
With every glimmer, fate's guide.

Whispers float on the golden rays,
Hopes interwoven in endless ways.
Tomorrow beckons with open arms,
To those who seek its shining charms.

Tracing Shadows on the Edge of Dreams

Tracing shadows where silence falls,
On the edge of dreams, the spirit calls.
Footsteps linger on pathways rare,
In whispers soft, the heart laid bare.

The night reveals a spectral dance,
Inviting wanderers to take a chance.
Through veils of twilight, spirits glide,
In the embrace where hopes abide.

Vision flickers, and passions spark,
Guiding souls through the endless dark.
Shadows weave a tapestry bright,
Amidst the currents of whispered light.

With every heartbeat, dreams take form,
In the night, where the wildflowers swarm.
Tracing shadows, we find our way,
Through the darkness to the break of day.

Moving closer, the dawn unfolds,
With promises wrapped in hues of gold.
On the edge of dreams, we'll forever stay,
Tracing shadows that never stray.

Veins of Nature's Embrace

In whispers low, the leaves confide,
With roots that weave, the earth's soft tide.
A tapestry of green, alive,
Where all the secret stories thrive.

The sun spills gold on every seam,
As flowers bloom, they chase a dream.
The songbirds sing a gentle tune,
Inviting hearts to pause, commune.

Cool streams flow with a tender grace,
Reflecting life in each embrace.
With every breeze, the branches sway,
In nature's arms, we wish to stay.

Mountains rise, a majestic frame,
While valleys whisper nature's name.
In every shadow, light shall dance,
A vibrant world, a fleeting chance.

Together we breathe, nature and I,
Under the vast, unfolding sky.
With every step, my spirit roams,
In veins of green, I find my home.

Echoes from the Twisted Canopy

Among the branches, stories weave,
In tangled tales, we dare believe.
The calls of distant birds take flight,
Echoes linger in fading light.

Mossy stones, a softened bed,
Where silent shadows softly tread.
The whispering winds know every word,
In forest depths, where thoughts are heard.

Gnarled roots form a knotted maze,
Guiding wanderers through a haze.
Each rustling leaf a secret shared,
In nature's heart, we are ensnared.

Through twisted limbs, the sunlight streams,
Awakening our hidden dreams.
Each sigh of dusk, a sacred vow,
As twilight's brush paints each branch now.

In every echo, wonder echoes,
Twisted tales where time bestows.
Nature's canvas, vast and grand,
Whispers of life, a steady hand.

Glimmers Where Branches Intertwine

In twilight's glow, the branches meet,
Creating paths where shadows greet.
A dance of leaves, a gentle sway,
Glimmers of light begin to play.

Where sunlight kisses tender skin,
Life's vibrant threads weave deep within.
Each tender shoot, a promise made,
A symphony in green and shade.

The air is rich with fragrant blooms,
Where every corner sweetly looms.
Beneath the arching boughs we roam,
In this vast green, we find our home.

With every step, the ground responds,
Echoing the beat of ancient bonds.
Together in this living shrine,
We listen close, where whispers shine.

As branches intertwine and bend,
A tapestry that has no end.
In every glimmer, life enshrined,
A world alive, forever kind.

Shadows Dancing on the Water's Edge

The sun dips low, the shadows stretch,
As ripples play at nature's sketch.
Upon the surface, magic swirls,
Where silent dreams and water twirls.

The moonlight weaves a silver thread,
To guide the night, where soft winds spread.
In gentle whispers, night unfolds,
Revealing tales the darkness holds.

Reflections shimmer, calm yet bright,
Dancing gently in fading light.
Each splash a note in evening's song,
A tranquil place where souls belong.

With every wave, a story sings,
Where time stands still and freedom clings.
Along the bank, the fireflies gleam,
In shadows dancing, we chase a dream.

As night embraces, shadows blend,
In nature's arms, we find our end.
With every heartbeat, spirit flows,
Along the edge, where magic grows.